Pebble® Plus
Bilingüe/Bilingual

Baila, baila, baila/Dance, Dance, Dance

Bailando ballet/ Ballet Dancing

por/by Kathryn Clay

Editora consultora/Consulting Editor: Gail Saunders-Smith, PhD

Asesora de contenido/Content Consultant: Heidi L. Schimpf
Directora de Programas y Servicios/Director of Programs and Services
Joy of Motion Dance Center, Washington, D.C.

CAPSTONE PRESS
a capstone imprint

Pebble Plus is published by Capstone Press,
151 Good Counsel Drive, P.O. Box 669, Mankato, Minnesota 56002.
www.capstonepub.com

 Books published by Capstone Press are manufactured with paper
containing at least 10 percent post-consumer waste.

Library of Congress Cataloging-in-Publication Data
Clay, Kathryn.
 [Ballet dancing. Spanish & English]
 Bailando ballet / por Kathryn Clay = Ballet dancing / by Kathryn Clay.
 p. cm.—(Pebble Plus bilingüe/bilingual. Baila, baila, baila/Dance, dance, dance)
 Includes index.
 Summary: "Simple text and photographs present ballet dancing, including
simple steps—in both English and Spanish"—Provided by publisher.
 ISBN 978-1-4296-5350-3 (library binding)
 1. Ballet—Juvenile literature. I. Title. II. Title: Ballet dancing. III. Series.
GV1787.5.C5318 2011
792.8—dc22   2010004183

Editorial Credits
Jennifer Besel, editor; Strictly Spanish, translation services; Veronica Bianchini, set designer;
 Eric Manske and Danielle Ceminsky, designers; Marcie Spence, media researcher;
 Sarah Schuette, photo stylist; Marcy Morin, scheduler; Laura Manthe, production specialist

Photo Credits
All photos by Capstone Studio/Karon Dubke

**The Capstone Press Photo Studio thanks Dance Express in
Mankato, Minnesota, and The Dance Connection in Rosemount,
Minnesota, for their help with photo shoots for this book.**

Note to Parents and Teachers

The Baila, baila, baila/Dance, Dance, Dance series supports national physical education
standards and the national standards for learning and teaching dance in the arts. This book
describes and illustrates ballet in both English and Spanish. The images support early readers
in understanding the text. The repetition of words and phrases helps early readers learn new
words. This book also introduces early readers to subject-specific vocabulary words, which are
defined in the Glossary section. Early readers may need assistance to read some words and to
use the Table of Contents, Glossary, Internet Sites, and Index sections of the book.

Table of Contents

Tabla de contenidos

All about Ballet

Point your toes, and turn in
a circle. It's fun to dance
ballet with friends.

Todo sobre el ballet

Pon los dedos de tus pies en punta
y gira en un círculo. Es divertido
bailar ballet con amigos.

Ballet uses movement to tell a story. Dancers need strong muscles to move smoothly.

El ballet usa el movimiento para contar un cuento. Los bailarines necesitan músculos fuertes para moverse suavemente.

What to Wear

Ballet dancers wear soft slippers.
Slippers bend easily to help dancers
point their toes.

Qué ropa usar

Los bailarines de ballet usan zapatillas de
baile. Las zapatillas se doblan fácilmente
para ayudar a los bailarines a poner
en punta los dedos de sus pies.

Dancers wear leotards and
tights when they practice.
They practice in studios.

Los bailarines usan mallas y
calzas cuando practican.
Ellos practican en estudios.

Dancers wear costumes or tutus for recitals. They perform recitals on big stages.

Los bailarines usan ropa para ballet o tutús para recitales. Ellos hacen los recitales en grandes escenarios.

Sweet Steps

Ballet has five positions.
Dancers learn where to hold
their arms and legs.

Pasos dulces

El ballet tiene cinco posiciones.
Los bailarines aprenden dónde
colocar sus brazos y piernas.

First/
Primera

Second/
Segunda

Third/
Tercera

Fourth/
Cuarta

Fifth/
Quinta

Ballet dancers bend their knees.

This move is called a plié.

_____

Los bailarines doblan sus rodillas.

Este movimiento se llama plié.

Say plié:
plee-AY

Di plié:
pli-é

Dancers balance on one foot.
Then they turn. This move is
called a pirouette.

Los bailarines mantienen
el equilibrio en un pie.
Luego giran. Este movimiento
se llama pirouette.

Say pirouette:
peer-ah-WET

Di pirouette:
pi-ru-et

Ready to Dance

Bend, turn, and jump

to the music.

Take a bow!

Listos para bailar

Flexiona, gira y salta

con la música.

¡Haz una reverencia!

Glossary

balance—to keep steady and not fall

leotard—a tight piece of clothing worn by dancers

muscle—a body part that pulls on bones to make them move

position—the way a dancer stands; ballet has five positions

recital—a show where people dance for others

studio—a room or building where a dancer practices

tutu—a short ballet skirt made of several layers of stiff net

Internet Sites

FactHound offers a safe, fun way to find Internet sites related to this book. All of the sites on FactHound have been researched by our staff.

Here's all you do:

Visit *www.facthound.com*

Type in this code: 9781429653503

Glosario

el equilibrio—permanecer sin moverse ni caerse

el estudio—un salón o edificio donde practican los bailarines

la malla—una prenda ajustada usada por los bailarines

el músculo—una parte del cuerpo que tira de los huesos para que se muevan

la posición—la manera en que se para un bailarín; el ballet tiene cinco posiciones

el recital—un espectáculo donde personas bailan para otras

el tutú—una falda para baile corta hecha de varias capas de tul rígido

Sitios de Internet

FactHound brinda una forma segura y divertida de encontrar sitios de Internet relacionados con este libro. Todos los sitios en FactHound han sido investigados por nuestro personal.

Esto es todo lo que tienes que hacer:

Visita *www.facthound.com*

Ingresa este código: 9781429653503

Index

Índice